THE

POLITICS

OF

MY

HEART

THE

POLITICS

OF

MY

HEART

WILLIAM

SLAUGHTER

Pleasure Boat Studio

FIRST PRINTING

Design by Shannon Gentry
Composition by Fred Elliott
Photographs (cover and author)
     by Jeanie Rini Slaughter

Printed in the United States of America
     by Thomson-Shore

Published by Pleasure Boat Studio
802 East Sixth
Port Angeles, WA 98362

Tel-Fax: (360) 452-8686
E-mail: pbstudio@pbstudio.com
URL: http://www.pbstudio.com

Library of Congress Cataloging-in-Publication Data

Slaughter, William, 1943–
     The politics of my heart / William Slaughter
        p. c.m.
     ISBN 0-9651413-0-6
     1. China—Poetry. I. Title
PS3569.L3844P6558 1996
     811'.54   96-68145

Acknowledgments

I am grateful to the United States Information Agency and the Council for the International Exchange of Scholars for the Senior Fulbright Lecturing Award at Beijing Foreign Studies University, 1987–88, that made my China writing possible; the University of North Florida for sabbatical leave, time and money; and the National Endowment for the Arts and the Jacksonville (Florida) Community Foundation for an Art Venture Grant that supported my return to China and the completion of this book.

Bakunin: "Death in China"

Cafe at St. Mark's: "Leave-Taking"

Connecticut Review: "Calligraphy Lesson" and "Old Chao"

Empty Bowl (poster poem): "How I Became a Daoist Monk"

Exquisite Corpse: "Street Life, Street Death," "Reporting from Beijing," "China's Last Lady," and "Last Chapter and Verse"

International Quarterly: "Reading Tiananmen Square"

JAMA (Journal of the American Medical Association): "Chinese Remedies"

Journal of American Studies (China): "Leave-Taking" and "New China Poem"

New Letters: "Walking the Corpse"

New York Quarterly: "Poem with Birds and Clocks"

Orbis (England): "What Chinese Men Have to Sing About"

Outposts (England): "Lines Written in China"

Passaic Review: "Laozi in Indiana"

Poetry: "Climbing Tai Shan"

Poetry East: "Professor Xu / Madame Bovary / Sparrow War"

The Prose Poem: "Toward a Border Crossing" and "Gulangyu"

People's Daily (Overseas Edition): "Poem with Birds
and Clocks" (in Chinese, trans. Li Gongzhao)

Rif/t: "Beijing Bird Men" and "The Man
Who Washed His Ears" (Shen Congwen)

UNTOLD STORIES (Empty Bowl): "Laozi in Indiana"
and "Leave-Taking"

World of English (China): "New China Poem," "How I Became
a Daoist Monk," and "Hungry Ghosts" (in English
and Chinese, trans. Wu Ningkun).

for Joey and Amy

Table of Contents

A Few Small Careful Strokes

The Hard Work of Memory

Until No Stone is Left

Poetry is a rival government
always in opposition to its cruder replicas.

William Carlos Williams
"The Basis of Faith in Art"

A

FEW

SMALL

CAREFUL

STROKES

New China Poem

Long flight, day lost,
well met. I wake
to greet the morning
in Beijing...
through Tokyo from L.A.
Outside my window,
the room
my Chinese friends
have given me,
I see
old men doing *taiji,*
their bodies more graceful,
agile, subtle,
than mine will ever be.
'You either make it
on the dance floor
or you don't make it.'
Well, then,
I don't make it.
Earth, as planet,
is dance... is floor.
Outside my window
I hear rooster crowing,
band saw sawing.
Workers
building New China.
Out of what?
Old lumber.
New China, new music.
I'll grow new ears,
learn to hear it.

But, for now,
I'll stay in,
read something old—
Confucius, the ANALECTS.
Discipline myself.
Go out later,
travel great distances,
visit Qufu.

How I Became a Daoist Monk

I made my way to China,
to Lao Shan
where, I had heard,
Daoist monks still lived,
but they didn't.

So there I was
all by myself
with no one to talk to,
nothing to do.

And there I still am
years later,
my beard turning white
like snow on the mountain.

It's all right.
I have patience enough
to wait for them,
the Daoist monks.

Expecting them
any day now,
I'm comfortable
with what I don't have,
believing everything.

So far as I know
I'm the only one.

Laozi in Indiana

Whatever it is
presents itself
to you,
accept it.
Beneficence
is at work
in the universe.
Live with it
awhile.
It has much
to teach you.
Patience
is its first
and second virtue.
Do not
spend yourself
carelessly.
It requires
nothing of you.
Be glad.
Patience
is its third
and last virtue.

Climbing Tai Shan

Six thousand steps,
'every step an arrival.'

On the way up, I'm thinking
...what to say when I pass
through the South Gate
to Heaven, as soon I must?

History has it
I'm supposed to say
something unforgettable,
wise. Confucius,
for example, looking down,
said: 'The world is small.'

At the Temple of Azure Clouds,
an old Chinese woman
with bound feet and walking
stick—a peasant woman,
a supplicant—appears to me.
Is she my mother?

Shall I say,
having climbed the mountain,
'I have climbed the mountain,'
am there, and will live
one hundred years?

The Han Emperor Wu,
who, twenty-one hundred
years ago, rejected
every manuscript
his writers submitted,
has a monument too:
a wordless, blank stone—
on which I can write anything,
the Emperor being dead.

Silence is unforgettable, wise.

Leave-Taking

for an old friend

Your own orient,
the one small room
you live in

with its usual litter
of Tang Dynasty
poems.

In the great tradition
we break bread
together

(for the last time)
and drink your best
and reddest

wine. We
remind ourselves
of the Chinese poets,

Du Fu...
and Li Bai who drowned
'trying to embrace

a moon'
in the Yangzi River.
A thousand years

separate them from us
and from each other.
Heroic death

is no longer possible.
The only rivers we have,
the only moons,

are those
that shine inside us
as rivers and moons

now and then
do. We drown in them
but return again

as Chinese poets
or mythological birds,
putting on

feathers
or pale, fragile,
thin bodies of poems.

And how
does the world
serve us in our prime?

With what
rewards are we met?
We bring our poems

back with us
for want of nourishment
in death, and console

ourselves with wine.
'At least we shall have
descendants,'

we say.
At least we shall have
our own small sons.

Lines Written In China

to a particular woman

If what Confucius
said was true,
that 'a woman
without talent

has virtue,'
then you, woman,
are without
virtue. Talent

has always meant
different things
to different men.
I, for one,

would like to know
what Confucius
would have said,
had he known you.

Sittings

in Chengdu, Sichuan

1.

Sitting in the Poem-Reciting Pavilion
—early spring, Year of the Dragon—
I'm remembering the Tang singing girl,
Xue Tao, whom I know

from SUNFLOWER SPLENDOR.
Her father died... too soon, before
she knew what a father's dying was for.
She used to live here. Without means,

her mother trained her for a life
that had language and love,
money and men, in it. And her life
did not disappoint

her mother's expectations.
Convince me otherwise: Physical beauty
is a bad idea. But Xue Tao was famous
for it. Provincial governors,

one by one, out from Beijing,
leveraging their futures, loved her
for it. But not one of them, ever,
mentioned her voice...

Xue Tao's voice, my reason
for remembering her. When she sang,
she sang. And her voice had a body
all its own. I love her for it.

Listening, I can still hear
—memory is my third ear—
the wine and the moon, the pillow
and the night that will never be

long enough... in her voice.
Will my wife, when she reads this,
be jealous, I hope so, of Xue Tao?
My twelve-hundred-year-old mistress.

2.

China has always gotten on...
slow time, my time. I'm not behind
here, where my wife is sitting
with her grudge, her only companion,
in the Grudge-Dissolving Pavilion.

But she's not getting into it,
she's not letting go of it. Hours ago,
on Renmin Lu, the People's Street,
my wife was robbed. But it wasn't
the People of China who robbed her.

It was just a man who had already lost
the only thing he ever had to spend:
the hard currency of his family name.
'Who steals my purse in China
pays me back with my own money.'

My wife knows how need can work a man
until he finally is what he doesn't have.
She doesn't need me to tell her...
eating bitterness isn't called for.
In China that is optional too.

Gulangyu

'Drum Wave Island'
off the south coast of China,
Fujian province. I've taken
a ferry across the Egret River
to get here. Beethoven

was always in love
in 1799, the year he wrote
his *Sonata Pathetique,*
from which I'm requesting
the adagio movement

for my funeral, music
to mourn by. Sunlight Cliff.
'The highest place we have,'
my Gulangyu friend says.
I'm standing on it.

Having climbed so high
I've earned the right
to look down and back
at the mainland. Distance
is what I've spent my life

trying for. Behind me
in the Lotus Flower Nunnery
there are no nuns on view,
only the traffic of the human
world far below. Beethoven,

at the end of his life,
heard differently, was deaf.
I haven't lost my hearing
yet, just my breath. As if
by request, a piano is playing,

somewhere in the distance,
a classical piece I recognize
but can't name. The notes
are giving themselves away
like family secrets

—the proudest houses—
in the island streets.
The heady air of the South
China Sea has dizzied me.
I still don't know

what my need is.
On my way up Sunlight Cliff
I passed a small cemetery.
The stones rose suddenly up.
It was there Beethoven

took me by surprise,
has kept me company
since. The stones
were unreadable; the lives
they marked, forgotten.

But desire is not gone.
Beethoven loved his mother
beyond measure. She died
too soon. He never married.
I'm with my wife on Gulangyu.

Poem with Birds and Clocks

The old woman
who lives
in a back lane
in Haidian
is not my mother.
We cannot speak
with each other
because
she is without
my language
as I am
without hers.
She keeps birds.
Nearby
is a clock factory
I have visited.
The workers there
are friendly
let me watch them
let me drink tea
with them.
They keep time
not birds.
The old woman
knows full well
with her pigeons
and her doves
that time
cannot be kept.

She invites me
with her hands
silently
eloquently
to sit down with her
pass time with her.
I cannot speak
with the workers
in the factory
either
who have hands
like clocks
and who do not
keep birds.

Chinese Remedies

Early morning
in Shanhaiguan,
the sun rising
from Bohai Bay.

Already
Barefoot Doctor
is out and about,
not walking

but riding...
a new bicycle.
Flying Pigeon,
color gray.

Business
must be good.
His saddle-bags
with red crosses,

strapped on
back, contain
everything—
from tiger bone

and rhino horn
to ginseng root
and bee pollen,
snake wine—

Village needs.
His patients
believe in him,
are feeling

better.
I find myself
believing too,
as I watch him

pedal to work,
make house-calls.
The heaviness
of night

falling away.
A new day,
like no other,
stretching us all.

Death in China

is part of life.
In Beijing,
the Northern Capital,
it happens like this:

One man pulls
another man's death-cart
through nameless streets
at dawn...

toward Babao Shan,
Eight Treasure Mountain,
where men, in the end,
have always gone.

Walking the Corpse

More than once
Farmer Li had imagined
himself dying, but always
at home in his own bed
surrounded by his children

and always
with his eyes open.
His wife was always there
too, in his imagining,
as were the necessary silks

and flowers. Always black.
And he had always liked,
especially, the picture
of himself, with the border
in black, hanging

above the empty box
that would have his ashes
in it soon. Forever.
Farmer Li had never
imagined himself dying

like this:
away from where he ate
and loved and slept
every night of his life.
He had never imagined

dying by day, responsibly,
at work in his own field.
Which is where the *ganshi*
who practice, in China,
the art of walking

the corpse back home
found him and bound him
to them. Farmer Li
would have been glad
of their skill

at making his death
look real, how he bowed,
spiritedly, to his neighbors
in passing. It would
almost have been worth it.

How I Got My Chinese Name

My Chinese friend, Shen Nan, gave it to me. Here's how.

When you give up your own alphabet, you give up a lot. You leave a lot behind. Like sound. When I look at English letters, I hear them; but when I look at Chinese characters, I don't. Only the silence that is in them for me.

William, Shen Nan says, my given name in English. It sounds foreign in her mouth. Associating freely, she decides on *Wei Yang,* and once again I am named.

Chinese is a tonal language, which is to say it speaks itself musically. It sings. The Chinese only have four hundred some different syllables to work with, but they keep changing the tones of those syllables so that an infinite variety of sounds—and meanings—is possible.

Basically, there are four tones. A favorite example in Chinese language texts is *ma:* neutral in the first tone, or no tone, voiced as *ma* and meaning "mother." In the second tone, rising, ma means "hemp" or "rope." *Ma,* falling and rising ambiguously in the third tone, means "horse." "Scold" is what *ma* in the fourth tone, falling, means; you have to be sure of yourself, or at least sound sure of yourself, to say it and be taken seriously.

Wei Yang—Wei in the fourth tone, *Yang* in the second—is no more a neutral or ambiguous name than Shen Nan is a neutral or ambiguous woman. No first or third tones for me. But it's not that simple; it never is in Chinese. And Shen Nan is not here to unconfuse me. I still have choices to make, she tells me, if I want to be able to write my name as well as say it. And I do; she promises to teach me how.

Every sound in Chinese can be represented by more than one character and each character means something quite different. So I have to choose which characters I want to represent *Wei* and *Yang;* therein lies my dilemma.

Wei, Shen Nan tells me, in the fourth tone, falling but sure of itself, can mean "ancient" or "glorious" if I choose one character; an army officer—high up, she says, but not a general; a captain maybe—if I choose another character; or "blue," the color not the mood, if I choose yet another. *Yang,* in the second tone, rising, can also mean many things and does, depending on which character I choose. It can mean the "sun," if I want it to, or something "foreign"... "exotic." *Yang* can mean a "sheep" too.

All I have to do to write myself in Chinese is choose my characters. I like the plural sound of that choosing. And it is enough for me to know that I can be, in Chinese, "Ancient Sun" or "Blue Sheep" or "Captain Exotic"... as my mood moves me. Thanks to Shen Nan.

Hungry Ghosts

All the men I've ever been
I still am. Hungry ghosts

are in me, each one
with his own name,

fault, apology, dream.
Every night, their mouths

open wide, and I feed them.
I always feed them.

Calligraphy Lesson

I have been
in China

long enough to know,
trusting my brush

is a foolish
thing to do...

in my late forties.
Sorrow and loss

are the very
ink I use,

which is fine,
black, and true.

Joy is too.
I have it

in my power
to name, *name,*

what I have lost
and wept for,

what gained.
But what good

would it do?
A man's character

is in his hand,
his life's work...

a few small
careful strokes.

THE

HARD

WORK

OF

MEMORY

Toward A Border Crossing

What's he thinking, I'm thinking, the real live Panda Bear?
As he rides his motor-bike around the ring in the Shanghai
Acrobatic Theater where he's a featured performer. With a
look, an air, of complacency about him. He's thinking
private thoughts. More than his trainer knows who turns in
the center of the ring pointing approvingly at the Panda
Bear. The trainer is completely taken in. He believes the
applause is for him. But the Panda Bear is nobody's fool.
He has an above average IQ and a diploma from Panda
Bear School. He has learned his China lesson well. His
eyes, and the expression on his face, reveal nothing. Give
nothing away. He's keeping it all in, saving it for himself.
The Panda Bear has a secret. One night—tonight?—he's
going to break the circle with his trainer still pointing
approvingly at him and ride his motor-bike out of the
theater into the night. He knows exactly what he's doing.
Who can stop him? The Panda Bear has done his home-
work. Has studied geography. The map of China is in his
head as he rides south out of Shanghai toward the border
crossing at Shenzhen. Panda Bears don't need passports to
get into the New Territories and Hong Kong. They just go.
He'll take up residence there in a small flat—in Stanley,
say—and live a quiet life anonymously. Perhaps he'll have
a stall on the waterfront where he'll sell small replicas of
himself which he'll draw with brush and ink using his own
right paw. Doing a tidy business. Smiling all the while.
Never looking back.

Street Life, Street Death

The streets of Beijing are not like the streets of any other city I've ever been in. Chinese pedestrians and cyclists, as I observe them in countless numbers—daily, nightly— on the streets of Beijing, live and die in what can only be called an ironic mode. A theater of the absurd.

Act One

I'm in a taxi, the Chinese version of a Mercedes sedan, on my way to Wangfujing, the principal shopping street in Beijing. A Chinese man, my age, walks—blindly, proudly—in front of the car. What's he thinking? I'm thinking. As the driver brakes, swerves... misses him, curses him. "He's not afraid to die." The pedestrian's manner—his carriage, his authority—suggests that he has missed too... the point. But he hasn't. He knows exactly what he's doing. By now, he has crossed the street and has gotten on to the next part of his life.

Act Two

I'm on a bus, the 332 bus, on my way to visit a friend at Beijing University. A Chinese woman, much younger than I am, astride her Flying Pigeon, refuses, steadfastly refuses, to yield the right of way, which is legally hers, as the bus turns toward her, aims at her. She doesn't hurry up; she doesn't slow down.

Rather, she behaves as if the bus is not there. And, for her, it isn't there. The bus stops. She stops it. And 80-odd passengers, including me, wait for her to pass. She passes.

Act Three

Acts One and Two repeat themselves, repeat themselves. Endlessly. Only sometimes, there are accidents. Deaths. My eyes have seen them. They're not pretty.

Why? Why do pedestrians and cyclists in Beijing, with such a great and physical handicap, take cars and buses on, head on? I've been asking myself that question, living here, and I think I have the answer.

Where, if anywhere, in post-Maoist China, do the Chinese feel free? In the streets... on foot and bike. The Chinese pedestrian and cyclist have the legal right of way and are not about to give it up. Challenging drivers is a sport and a pastime for them, as bull-fighting was for Hemingway. Death in the afternoon. To put one's anonymous self at risk in these streets is to earn the right to one's name. After all that fear and hiding, after all those campaigns.

"I'm Nobody. Who are you? Are you Nobody too? Good! Then there are a billion of us. Don't tell." But walking to the free market or cycling home from work, a Chinese man or woman can be Somebody... can stop a car or a bus, can make people wait. Attention must be paid.

Something like a psychological equivalent of the territorial imperative is expressing itself in the streets of Beijing. Tennessee Williams defined "desire," a favorite word of his, as a man's wanting to have more space than the world has given him to occupy. The anonymous Chinese pedestrian or cyclist, being one-billionth of New China, wants more space. And is staking his or her claim in the streets. As a free agent. With style, with grace under pressure. Every play a power play.

35

Beyond all that heavy language, there's the plain and simple fact of the rush one gets from living near death. I know, having just purchased a Phoenix—I like the symbol; I like the name—and having taken, myself, to the streets of Beijing. When I'm not riding, I'm walking the streets of New China, feeling free, in my New Balance shoes. I brought them with me. I didn't leave everything behind.

Chinese Bicycle Poem

Phoenix, Black Rooster,
Gold Lion, Five Rams, Flying
Pigeon, Forever.

Beijing Bird Men

are beautiful,
unlikely and strange
as the word is,
having to do with men.
They have retired,
as in China
by law at sixty
they must,
but they are not old.
Late in the afternoon
in a brown city
they come together
in parks without names,
wherever green is.
Beijing bird men
no longer
have drowsy emperors
to keep awake,
but still their birds,
with soft beaks
in bamboo cages,
sing. Still they sing.
Nightingales,
like the city,
are brown.
I did not know that,
never having seen
one before.
Beijing bird men
swing them,

with soft beaks
in bamboo cages,
by hooks from trees
or with their arms,
giving them
'a sense of flight.'
Air is heaven,
an exercise yard.
There is metaphor
here, song
competing with song.
Something cultural,
revolutionary.
But I resist it.

What Chinese Men Have to Sing About

Chinese men,
when they are by themselves,
sing. Quietly, softly,

they sing. As if words
were secrets in their mouths,
as if they were innocent,

like boys whose voices
have not yet changed.
I, who have read

what they have lived
and have their history
by heart, know

that Mao freed them twice.
Once in 1949 at Liberation,
and again in 1976 when,

mercifully, he died.
I, who do not know
what they have to sing about

unless it is just that.

Reporting from Beijing

China Daily, the "English-Language Newspaper" here, reviewed—in its March 10, 1988, issue—an exhibit of the young, he's 31, Chinese sculptor, Wu Shaoxiang, at the China Art Gallery, "the most prestigious art gallery in the country." The review was positive, supportive; it even lauded Wu's work, referring to him as "one of the pioneers of China's modern sculpture" and noting that it is "not surprising now" that the China Art Gallery is open to "foreign modern abstract art." It seems Wu's "break-throughs" include using "deformed and exaggerated female bodies as his basic language," using color, which is "almost nonexistent in contemporary Chinese sculpture," and using "such daily objects as rope, clocks and shoes" in his work. You get the picture; or rather, you get the sculpture.

I saw Wu's exhibit, with my own "foreign" eyes, before not after I read the *China Daily* review. And what I saw, one of his pieces, is with me still, and always will be, in my mind. Let me describe it for you—ironically, in words—from bottom to top. I say "it," because the piece remains nameless, appropriately without title, in my mind. On the floor, a stack of Chinese magazines, tightly bound with rope and painted red. On top of the magazines, a stack of Chinese books, tightly bound with rope and painted red. On top of the books, a head, a wooden head, a dummy's head, perfectly round and painted white... with enormous lips painted red, stitched shut with white thread.

That's "it." I'm thinking of what red paint meant during the Cultural Revolution, what it was splashed on. China's books. Her poets and scholars ruined, their lips stitched shut.

Fay Zwicky, an Australian writer of poems and stories, had a dream her first night in Beijing. Her reason for being here: a Conference on Australian Studies in China. She was an "invited" guest, so as to distinguish her, I suppose, from the "uninvited" guests—of which, so far as I know, there weren't any. The conference took place—in March of this year, 1988—on the campus of "my" university, Beijing Foreign Studies University, where I teach. I had nothing to do, personally, with the conference, but the Australian writers, who did, stayed in "my" guest house, the so-called Foreign Experts' Guest House, where I live.

So I met Fay Zwicky, a happy meeting. And she told me, over breakfast, the morning after she had it, her dream. As I remember her telling it, here it is:

> *Somebody—I don't know who—presents me*
> *with myself. But I'm not myself. I'm a baby.*
> *And I'm holding this baby and I'm looking*
> *at it. It's beautiful... not like me at all.*
> *And it has a long throat, like a lizard's,*
> *green and translucent. And I'm looking*
> *into its mouth when, suddenly, I notice,*
> *it has no tongue.*

A baby that won't cry, a baby that can't cry. Fay was already, she said, feeling "dislocated" and "restrained" in China. Her words, not mine. There are walls around everything in China. Some you can see, some you can't. But they're there... just the same.

Jeanie, my wife, has been listening to a tape of Philip Bailey's song "Chinese Wall" a lot lately. There's a line in it, "lips that burn but do not speak," silences me every time I hear it. In class, my students "do not speak." Every day I have less to say. I've been in China seven months.

Men Who Washed Their Ears

1.

Old Chao

Old Chao never had any big ideas,
only small ones. Perhaps that's why
his Emperor, Yao, liked him.
Old Chao didn't earn his reputation
as a wise man by studying Confucius
and passing his examinations,
or by lying awake at night worrying,
or by lecturing under an apricot tree
brilliantly. Old Chao
earned his reputation differently.
By climbing an apricot tree
and taking up residence there,
by refusing steadfastly
to say or do anything else,
by breathing knowledge in like air.
Emperor Yao soon tired of governing,
his power having thinned like his hair.
And liking Old Chao,
he called on him, made him offers,
with all his tongues working.
'The dragon throne, the dragon throne.
I'll give you everything. My daughters.'
Emperor Yao's words
blew through Old Chao's tree
like no wind at all, and with a bowl
of pure spring water, ritually,
Old Chao washed his ears, heard nothing.

2.

for Shen Congwen, 1902-1988,
one of China's greatest writers,
and his people...

Shen Congwen, the same man,
who wrote books in China all his life
no matter what was in them
so long as he believed it.
Who said: 'I never believed in power.
Wisdom is more important.'
Who was made to suffer
during the Cultural Revolution.
Who was punished for his books.
Shen Congwen, the same man,
who was 'rehabilitated' by Chairman Mao
who had a different plan for him,
who called him in and 'invited' him
to write for the people.
Shen Congwen, the same man,
who had given himself in China all his life
to writing for the people.
Who heard Chairman Mao out
and said: 'Isn't it nice to be in demand.'
The same man who washed his ears
and wrote nothing ever again.
Power, wisdom. Shen Congwen.

Where Confucius Is

Qing Ming Festival Poem

I am writing this
in Qufu,
a small town
in Shandong Province,
home to Confucius
living, home
to Confucius dead.
I am writing this
at his burial place
in a forest
of cypress and pine
—in New China
the last
of its kind?
Ancestor worship
is 'feudal practice'
in New China,
is condemned.
But the Revolution
did not change
everything. New
Chinese still feed
their dead.
You can tell
who a man
is, in New China,
his station in life,
by how he eats.

But no banquet
has been
set for Confucius,
where he is.
At his stone
table, which is
empty, I am
an uninvited guest.
Let Confucius eat.

Professor Xu / Madame Bovary / Sparrow War

Without his wife,
who drowned her name
in No Name Lake,
1968,

Professor Xu
is still himself.

Just now
in a small courtyard
—his memory garden,
he calls it—
among sunflowers
taller than he is,
the only
private property
history has left him,

Professor Xu is doing
what he has always done
there. He is

remembering...
his student days
in France
before the Great War.
(There have been
so many lesser wars
since.) How
he learned the language
reading Flaubert.

Language...
a cracked kettle
on which we beat out
tunes for bears
to dance to,
while all the time
we long to move
the stars to pity.

As Professor Xu
remembers it,
Chairman Mao declared
one of those lesser wars
on China's sparrows,
1956...

Listening
with his inner ears,
he hears his countrymen
making political noises
on cracked kettles
too, until
the sparrows, guilty
of eating China's grain,
fall to earth, exhausted.

Home. Where is home?

Professor Xu, longing
in his 'memory garden,'
is home.

An innocent sky
full of sparrows
by day
and stars by night...
unmoved by language,
without pity. Is home.

Professor Xu, loving
Emma Bovary like a wife.

Sentences for Jiang Qing

1.

China's Last Lady

Jiang Qing
one of the gang
Mao's widow
his fourth wife
who never really
lived with him
after Liberation
in 1949
has outlived
herself
is ready to die
but life for her
goes on for her
in Qin Cheng
a prison not far
from Beijing
where she has
a room of her own
but not much
is left for her
not movies not
lovers not China
only rag dolls
she sews
for children
she never sees

knowing that
face in China
is self is pride
and saving it
a career
I wonder
if before she
sews the buttons
on for eyes
the smiling
mouth the nose
those dolls
she ever sees
a child's face
her own face
innocent
and confesses
all at once
her guilt
how without
intending to
she became
the Chairman's dog
when he told her
to bite she bit
and just
for a second
regretted it
all her country
men and women
hurt lost
gone dead

2.

Last Chapter and Verse

A woman of many callings...
Li Jin was her birth name,
'Used Shoe.' From her father,
a carpenter, she inherited
her proletarian feet.

Li Yunhe, a man teacher
called her, 'Cloud Crane.'
She was young, tall, thin.

An opera singer in Wuning,
she called herself
—for no known reason—
'Blue Apple,' Lan Ping.

But it was Mao himself
who named her Jiang Qing,

the night she came
like a line of Tang poetry,
a 'Lapis River,' bluer than blue,
into his Yanan cave.

...

In the beginning was the end.
'Let me dissect myself before you,'
she once said, quoting Lu Xun.
But she never did.

Not even in her last chapter
and verse she left behind
for Deng Xiaoping,
that 'little bottle' of a man.
That 'braggart king,'

she called him
in the death note she wrote.
'Don't feel happy too soon.
You will not have a good death.'

The only stones she had,
her words, she aimed at him.
Blaming him for everything,

on May 14, in Qin Cheng,
China's Prison Number One,
with her own belt she hanged
herself…

and felt,
for the first and last time,
beyond her need
'to turn grief into strength,'
the unbearable weight
of history, her heavy heart.

The Woman on the Bridge

near where I live in Beijing
is mad. I know she is.
How many times have I passed her by,
wondering who told her to stay there,
and why?
As if she had instructions
and were following them exactly,
as if she were official. Which she is.
Her office is forgetting.
Already she has forgotten everything
that has happened to her, and to China,
since 1968 when...
She can't remember.
Her eyes see but they don't see
out or in. Surfaces only.
History emptying itself out of her head.
The woman on the bridge is mad.
She doesn't even know her own secrets.

Walking Backwards in Beijing

'lost inside himself'
How ready the phrase is
and empty
until I attach it
to the old man alone
I see passing by
my gate
on the Third Ring Road
every day at the same time
just before the sun rises.
I get up early
so as not to miss him,
as if he were
my invited guest.
What attracts me
and holds me to him
is the inescapable fact
that he is walking
backwards
and seeming
not to notice anything
different in his city.
Perhaps he spent
the first half of his life
conducting his affairs
like everyone else,
moving forward only
with great purpose.
But now,
what can I say?
The principle of balance
is at work in the universe?

'yin and yang'
Somehow everything
turns and evens out
in the end.
The last half of his life,
which presumably
he is in,
the old man alone,
walking backwards
as he does
on the Third Ring Road,
compensates himself
for time and love
already lost.
Not knowing him
at all really, and never
having heard his story,
I am less than sure
and can only guess
at his reasons.
Has he assigned himself
the hard work of memory?
So as to have
another life, live twice,
and find inside himself
again the wife
or son or daughter
that circumstance
or death
has taken from him.
Without knowing why
he is feeling crowded
and has yet to notice me.

UNTIL

NO

STONE

IS

LEFT

Reading Tiananmen Square

The text of Tiananmen Square, which is still being read, was written communally. Re-presenting a small part of it here, I have set translations of Chinese poems— written by students, by citizens, who were involved in the Pro-Democracy Movement during the Beijing Spring of 1989—like jewels, however rough their cut, in a narrative ring of my own prose. The poems from Tiananmen were written as *dazi bao:* "big character posters," expressions of the great heart of the Chinese people. They were posted in and around the Square—on walls, in tunnels—but they were unsigned. After June 4, Bloody Sunday, when the People's Liberation Army moved against the people, they were collected, faxed to Pro-Democracy supporters in Hong Kong, and from there to Taiwan, where they found American poet Mike O'Connor who translated them.

The poems from Tiananmen are what their translator has called documentary poems, or "docu-poems." Beyond the monitoring of CNN and other television networks, the Square was wired in the Spring of 1989. "Small Questions," "Fasting," "Mad Woman," "China," and other docu-poems got out of Beijing over the wire. Whatever else they are, they are electric poems, both literally and figuratively. They record, in language charged by the historical moment of their writing, what it felt like to be there, Chinese and alive. "The body electric" that Walt Whitman sang in the middle of his century has taken on a different meaning at the end of our century. The small part of the text of Tiananmen Square that I am re-presenting here sings the body, and soul, electric of the Chinese people. Against the bullets of the People's Liberation Army, these poems were, and are, cast like ballots.

The Politics of My Heart

There is a cliche among foreigners in China that goes like this: "When you have been in China for a week, you think you have a book to write. When you have been in China for a month, you think you have an article to write. When you have been in China for a year, you know you have nothing to write." I am not a sinologist. I do not have the language, Chinese—only enough of it to survive there, to get by on the street. But my politics, having to do with China, are informed. They are the politics of my eyes and ears; they are the politics of my heart.

My wife, Jeanie, says: "Either we should never have gone to China... or we should never have come back from China." In fact, we are not all the way back. Not yet, not ever. China will not leave us alone. We love China in much the same way that Bai Hua does in his banned-in-China film, *Bitter Love*. We love it bitterly, ironically.

My reading of Tiananmen Square is made up of "slivers" of language. I call them slivers because China has gotten under my skin, and because China hurts.

Small Questions

Child: Mama Mama these young aunties and uncles,
    why aren't they eating anything?
Mother: They wish to receive a beautiful gift.

Child: What gift?
Mother: Freedom.

Child: Who will give them this beautiful gift?
Mother: They themselves.

Child: Mama Mama in the Square,
     why are there so many people?
Mother: It is a holiday.

Child: What holiday?
Mother: The holiday of lighting of the torch.

Child: Where is the torch?
Mother: Inside the hearts of us all.

Child: Mama Mama Who is riding in the ambulance?
Mother: A hero.

Child: Why is the hero lying down?
Mother: To best let the child behind him see.

Child: Am I that child?
Mother: Yes.

Child: To see what?
Mother: The flower with petals every color
     of the rainbow.

Quotations from Napoleon, Mao, and Others

"China is a sleeping giant," Napoleon once said; the Chinese themselves often quote him. "When she wakes, she will shake the world." What nightmare did the students find themselves waking from during the most recent Beijing Spring? What wishes unfulfilled attracted them to, and held them in, Tiananmen Square?

Chairman Mao: *Zaofan you li.* "To rebel is justified." To the Red Guard in Tiananmen Square. August 18, 1966.

Chairman Mao: "Don't challenge a rattlesnake... unless you can chop its head off." An old Chinese saying that he appropriated as his own.

Question: "What's the news today?" Answer: "The news is that one point one billion Chinese hearts are dead." A conversation, reported in his TIANANMEN DIARY, between Harrison Salisbury and a Chinese student in Tiananmen Square the morning after.

"As long as there shall be stones, the seeds of fire will not die." Lu Xun, one of the greatest Chinese writers of our century.

What the Students Knew

They knew that China had long suffered from political mood swings of the most violent kind, that she had acquired—no, that she had induced in herself—over the years, especially since 1949, something like cultural schizophrenia, alternating periods, or cycles, of liberation and repression.

In Chinese, the characters *fang* and *shou,* usually rendered in English as "expansion" and "contraction," suggest this. Every opening by the government, meaning the Party, of China's door—not only to the world outside but to her own people—was always followed, they knew, sooner rather than later, by yet another closing (even slamming) of that same door. And the people, they knew, who accepted the Party's repeated invitation to pass through that door—if not to freedom, then to a freer existence—paid dearly for it, having put everything, including their very lives, at risk.

Fasting

1.

Banners—Flags—Flying—Spreading
Inside hope lives the seed of despair, and inside despair
    lives hope.

Fasting   Fasting   Fasting
There has never been a word   as strong as that word
        today.

2.

Fasting is a shout of despair,
            and the most unshakable protest
Fasting is the frailest power, and the most dogged struggle
Fasting is light   piercing the darkness, piercing the night
Fasting is heat   the warmth of the soil,
            the warmth of the rice sprout
Fasting is fire   lighting up slogans, lighting up banners
Fasting is lightning   cutting through apathy and paralysis
Fasting is thunder   jarring the bloodstream,
            jolting the heart
Fasting is wind   stirring up dark clouds,
            stirring up our people
Fasting is love   of our country, of our people
Fasting is hatred   of our impoverishment
            and backwardness
Fasting is anxiety   when does it soar,
            when does it abruptly arise
Fasting is ill-will   always fraught with disaster
            and calamity

3.

Behind me are the bones of the people's heroes
Commemorative stone guiding the ship of state
From the beginning of being   from the beginning
        of courage
From the beginning of sacrifice to the gods
        from the beginning of death
The monument has stood here in silence.
The monument has vigilantly stood at the backs
        of the people

Reminding them to be calm and firm of purpose
Every time there is a wavering
The ship of state becomes more bewildered
Every time there is a wavering
The ship of state pitches and rolls.

Zhong and Guo

Zhong and *guo* are the characters that, put together,
mean China: *Zhong / Guo,* the Middle Kingdom. The
Chinese are a wonderfully superstitious people, great
believers in the old high art of geomancy: divining the
future by unearthing and tracing out lines of force. And all
the lines of force in "New" China intersect in Tiananmen
Square—the middle, as it were, of the Middle Kingdom.
For the Chinese, a powerful, charged, magnetic place, a
kind of psycho-cultural force field.

Tiananmen Square is said to be the biggest public
square in the world—bigger, for example, than either Red
Square in Moscow or St. Peter's in Rome. And in its
middle, of course, is Chairman Mao's tomb, his monolithic
mausoleum. I paid it, paid him, a ritual visit—out of...
was it curiosity or perversity?—during my own Beijing
Spring of 1988. Mao's corpse lies there, in the middle of
the middle of the Middle Kingdom, as it were, in an
hermetically sealed glass coffin, on view. My eyes have
seen it, still heavy with meaning for China's future.

Walking across Tiananmen Square

I was walking across Tiananmen Square in the early
spring of 1988, working on a small poem in my head. By
then, I had been in China for a while and had begun to
lose at least some of my peculiarly American innocence.
But, unlike many of my foreign (as in: not Chinese)

friends, who blamed the SYSTEM for everything that was missing from their lives in China, deprivations they did not suffer gladly, I really liked living there.

My poem was my own version of a "Self-Criticism," a much practiced genre in recent Chinese writing. The Party requires self-criticisms of its erring members; Public Security requires them of erring citizens—and even, though infrequently, of erring foreigners. Confession, whether it is good for the soul or not, is a particularly useful survival technique in China. Mine, in my head, sounded like this:

> I can't help myself.
> I like this city Mao
> is dead in. Sorry.

I did like Beijing, and I still do. But I was not sorry about Mao. I was wrong about him. Tiananmen Square proved that. He is not dead. His ghost is still everywhere to be found in China—a haunting presence.

Mao's Ghost

Mao was in Tiananmen Square himself that day. Not just in my head, not just in my poem. His picture still hangs over the gate of Heavenly Peace, which—by the way—is a literal translation of the Chinese characters *tian/an/men*. The Gate of Heavenly Peace is the entrance to the Forbidden City, the Imperial Palace from which China was ruled, by one dynasty or another, for centuries. Above that gate, and picture, on October 1, 1949, from a reviewing stand which is still there, Mao proclaimed victory in his first revolution and announced the existence of his New China. And on August 18, 1966, from the same stand, he faced one million Chinese youths, named them the Red Guard, and charged them with bringing off the

Great Proletarian Cultural Revolution, his second
revolution: "an episode in the history of Man's inhumanity
to man," Anne F. Thurston says, in ENEMIES OF THE
PEOPLE, "surpassed only by the Nazi holocaust, the
Stalinist purges, and the recent genocide in Cambodia."

Mad Woman

All day long hidden in the box called China
      washing diapers   for thousands of years
Now   I spread apart my own bones and flesh
Beat them into a metal knife   slash the disgusting faces
      of this world
The disgusting faces of these men.

China   a father who killed his own sons
And this night, molested his daughters   China   China
A living coffin   in which I have been buried
      for a thousand years
My breasts   have become my own tomb
The whole length of my body   grown over with lichen
      and moss.

Corpses overflow this nation   My naked body soaks in
The pus and blood   flowing thick on the Yellow
      and Yangzi rivers   for thousands of years
They cannot wash white my skin
I lie in bed   weeping and caressing myself,
      abusing myself
China   These proper and respectable men
      always disappoint me.

In thousands of years   only I, one person, have climbed
      out of this living coffin
Abandoning the pervading boredom and death   smashing
      the darkness

My black eyes   black hair   black-colored skirt and blouse
Black-feet   and black, black soul
Only my gloves are white
This one pair of white gloves can be enough to kill
        our father.

I am an hysterical Chinese woman
The first mad woman   but so what
In the midnight hour   I run away from home
Casting off my own husband
But so what.

I am a mad woman   not a stitch of clothing on
Standing in a treetop,   searching for the sun
At the places where men vote   I am the opposing ballot
But so what.

Throughout the land the nation's farmers
The nation's small-town people
And the bureaucrats
Have come from innumerable wars
From thousands of years of history, and in so much time
        have not been rescued
At the intersection of death   in the earth's anatomy
They have gone from slavery to slavery
Their arms, once wrenched counter-clockwise, finally drop
        like roll-curtains
And change into plants.

Newspapers founded on lies
And the Great Wall founded on ashes are the same
Refined and gentle scholars   old men reluctant
        to be buried
And the insouciant, I-don't-give-a-damn young men
        are the same
Famous poets squatting in public johns
        and the computer kids are the same

Tea houses, spread out and numerous as stars,
    and the offices of research institutes are the same
I hate everything   Confucius   Zhuangzi
    Stalin   Marx
They make me sick   I want to swallow all falsehood
    and crime
I died   I took flight   and couldn't race
    toward the moon of immortality
The filthy China night   body tattooed with stars
Like an adulterous man   lies face downward
    on my shoulders
Humiliating my lover   I want to kill you
From now on   you can't pollute my body
I am not a mad woman   I'm a human being
    and am willing to suffer my punishment.

Intellectuals in China

    The China the students in Tiananmen Square during the most recent Beijing Spring had inherited was—under whatever cover, in whatever disguise—still, essentially, Mao's China. And their teachers have remembered for them what that means.

    But Mao did not invent the banned book—or, for that matter, the whispered word—in China; Qin Shi Huang, the first emperor of the Qin Dynasty in the third century B.C., from whom China takes its name, did. Not only is Qin Shi Huang credited as the founder, the unifier, of modern China, completing the Great Wall and standardizing the written language, but also he is credited, ironically, with having ordered the burning of books and the burying of intellectuals alive. Mao has often been compared, by the intellectuals themselves, to Qin Shi Huang, and he is even said to have bragged: "Yes, we are Qin Shi Huang, Qin Shi Huang. But Qin Shi Huang only killed several hundred intellectuals. We have killed several hundred thousand."

Intellectuals in China and their books have had, at best, an ambiguous relationship to power, as it has bodied itself forth in the Party or State. During the Cultural Revolution, which can only be described, looking back at it, as "a failure of morality," in Harold Laswell's words, "a rupture of conscience," the universities were either closed—shut down—or changed in ways that made them unrecognizable as themselves. For example, the liberal arts disappeared altogether, whole departments gone: political science, sociology, anthropology, philosophy, logic, and history. Whole disciplines abolished. Teachers and students alike were subjected to humiliating and painful struggle sessions; confined in "cow sheds" or "cattle pens" with little food and no medical care; or sent out to the countryside for "re-education through manual labor," like carrying night-soil to the fields, in a May Seventh Cadre School.

China

His hand begins to prepare for attack
Amputating my legs to the groin   throwing my head
        to the execution grounds
The children still breathe in schoolrooms
Numberless office doors open and close
Those with a vote share a consensus   chat,
        read newspapers, drink tea
These slaves were already modernized, early
My freedom has been stolen   locked in a clothes closet
        with mildew and underwear
And the classic poet has been killed by the moon
        and dares not rise again.

The sun suddenly goes mad   already there is no road
        for my escape

The people crowd tightly together   the freeways flow
       in four directions
Directly, I am forced to enter a single hotel-room   FEAR
I am placed in the black night where history's heroes scream
Give myself oxygen, strap on a straitjacket
The venetian blinds recoil   take comfort in my evil plight.

My four limbs become stainless-steel tubes   wiped
       so clean by them
My eyes are blinded   plucked out like corks   afloat
       with the wastepaper
Layer upon layer of emptiness   this is my daily
       knocking of rice bowl and chopsticks
Unquestionably   the black night has come
I cannot build the stars   or deal perfunctorily
       with my body,
That wound and the dawn which cannot be healed
My face is not the face of a farmer,
       but it has the same resemblance to the land
The Square fell to the enemy   in the south   I stayed
       overnight in a cheap hotel
The smell of seafood in the streets made me sick
I really wish I had died with the citizens.

Until No Stone is Left

     Statues of Chairman Mao are everywhere in China.
He had them built to scale, which is to say: They are
magnified, as his sense of himself as the Last Emperor was,
out of all proportion. In the spring of 1988, I was in
Chengdu, the capital of Sichuan province, for a Fulbright
Conference. Walking about, I found myself in the center of
the city, surrounded by municipal buildings, done in the
Russian style of the 1950s, and in the presence of yet
another statue of Chairman Mao. But this one was different;

this one was scaffolded, as if something were about to happen to it. I wondered what and started writing "Until No Stone is Left."

On the same day, all over China, scaffolds go up and tarpaulins come down around the remaining statues of Chairman Mao—erected by Chairman Mao, in honor of Chairman Mao —the Great Helmsman. We know that something is going on in there, but we don't know what... looking on in wonder. My guess is as good as any. Deng Xiaoping has retired, but Deng Xiaoping has not retired. He is still China's puppet-master; he still pulls China's strings. When Deng dies—he's in his eighties— all over China, on the same day, the tarpaulins will be lifted, the scaffolds removed. And lo! Chairman Mao will have become... Deng Xiaoping. Even as I write this, the workers are chipping away at Mao with their hammers and chisels. Deng is a smaller man than Mao was. 'He's in there somewhere, we know he is.' We hear the workers say, chipping away. What I conclude from this is: China's next 'real' leader will have to be a smaller man than Deng Xiaoping, and Deng Xiaoping is a small man, so the workers can still chip away stone and get at him. As the people in China get bigger, the leaders get smaller. Until no stone is left, until they're not there. At all.

Notes

A Few Small Careful Strokes

"New China Poem." *Taiji* is the art of shadow boxing, a form of exercise practiced by Chinese, old and young, especially in the early morning. Qufu is "a small town / in Shandong Province, / home to Confucius / living, home / to Confucius dead." See my poem "Where Confucius Is." The teachings of Confucius (551?–479 B.C.) are known as the ANALECTS.

"Laozi in Indiana." Laozi is regarded as the founder of Daoism. His dates are 604?–531 B.C. His book is the DAODEJING. In Mandarin Chinese Laozi means "old master."

"Climbing Tai Shan." Tai Shan in Shandong Province is perhaps the most revered of China's sacred mountains. It has Daoist associations. Pilgrims climb it, all six thousand steps, with the help of the Daoist powers and presences that reside in temples, such as the Temple of Azure Clouds, on the mountain-top. The monument to the Han Emperor Wu is one of many monuments and shrines there too.

"Leave-Taking." Du Fu and Li Bai were Chinese poets of the Tang Dynasty (618–907 A.D.). "Trying to embrace / a moon / in the Yellow River" is Ezra Pound's explanation, in his "Epitaph," of Li Bai's death by drowning. But Chinese legend has it that Li Bai drowned, in the manner and for the reason that Pound describes, in the Yangzi not the Yellow River… at Dangtu, Anhui Province. "At least we shall have / descendents" is a line from Kenneth Rexroth's translation of Du Fu's poem "To Pi Ssu Yao," which is in his ONE HUNDRED POEMS FROM THE CHINESE (New Directions: New York, 1971), 15.

"Lines Written In China." In the Confucian ranking system, women were subordinate to men. "We should not be too familiar with the lower orders or with women," Confucius is reported to have said. See Alasdair Clayre in THE HEART OF THE DRAGON (Houghton Mifflin: Boston, 1975), 83.

"Sittings." 1. SUNFLOWER SPLENDOR is an anthology of "Three Thousand Years of Chinese Poetry," edited by Wu-Chi Liu and Irving Yucheng Lo (Indiana University Press: Bloomington, 1975). Xue Tao (768–831 A.D.) is, according to Eric W. Johnson who did the notes on her for Liu and Lo, "the most famous woman poet of the Tang dynasty" (564). The old spelling of her name, Hsüeh T'ao, is used in SUNFLOWER SPLENDOR. 2. Chinese use the phrase "eating bitterness" to describe the ability to survive hardship with dignity and pride.

"Poem with Birds and Clocks." Haidian is a district in northwest Beijing, much of it made up of *hutongs,* back lanes and alleyways winding through old neighborhoods.

"Chinese Remedies." Shanhaiguan is the village in Hebei Province where the Dragon Head of the Great Wall drinks from the Yellow Sea which, as the land encloses it, is known as Bohai Bay.

"Death in China." Beijing translates into English as "the Northern Capital," Babao Shan as "Eight Treasure Mountain." Babao Shan is the official cemetery on the western outskirts of Beijing.

"Walking the Corpse." "It is important to Chinese to die at home... In earlier days, in some parts of China, there was even a tradition called *ganshi*—walking the corpse back home. So important was it to die at home that a person who died on the road was actually walked home, as though he were alive, the skill of those whose occupation it was to lead the corpse being measured by how realistic the movements of the corpse appeared." Anne F. Thurston, ENEMIES OF THE PEOPLE (Harvard University Press: Cambridge, 1988), 150.

"Hungry Ghosts." Hungry ghosts are still felt presences in China, and they are very powerful. See, for example, the explanation of *Qing Ming* in my note on "Where Confucius Is."

"How I Got My Chinese Name." Shen Nan's father, Shen Zuoyao, is a renowned calligrapher. He carved the chop with which this book is sealed.

The Hard Work of Memory

"Toward a Border Crossing." Shenzhen is both a boom town and a Special Economic Zone (SEZ) set up to encourage and promote the transfer of technology and the investment of foreign capital in mainland China. It is situated in Guangdong Province on the border between mainland China and the New Territories, which are part of the mainland but were leased to Great Britain, along with Hong Kong, in 1898. Stanley, once a fishing village on the south coast of Hong Kong Island, is now a small residential community popular with Westerners.

"Chinese Bicycle Poem." Phoenix, Black Rooster, Gold Lion, Five Rams, and Forever are, in fact, the brand names of Chinese bicycles.

"What Chinese Men Have to Sing About." In China Liberation is what the victory of the Communists over the

Nationalists is officially called. Chairman Mao proclaimed that victory and the birth of a nation, New China, on October 1, 1949. He died on September 9, 1976.

"Reporting from Beijing." Fay Zwicky's most recent collection, to my knowledge, is POEMS 1970–1992 (University of Queensland Press: Brisbane, 1992).

"Men Who Washed Their Ears." 1. "Old Chao." Alasdair Clayre tells a version of the Old Chao and Emperor Yao story in THE HEART OF THE DRAGON (239). "Washed his ears" is a phrase Chinese use to describe not a man's refusal to listen but his refusal to hear. 2. "Shen Congwen." Shen Congwen wrote about "his people"—the Yuan River people of the border region where the provinces of Sichuan, Hunan, and Guizhou meet in China's west—in his many books, such as BORDER TOWN & OTHER STORIES (China Books: San Francisco, 1981) and RECOLLECTIONS OF WEST HUNAN (University of Washington Press: Seattle, 1982).

"Where Confucius Is." *Qing Ming* is a traditional festival, the date of which is determined, every spring, by the ancient lunar calendar. It is the occasion of the Chinese honoring—and appeasing—their ancestral dead by sweeping clean their graves and feeding their hungry ghosts. "For to Chinese, food is an obsession. When Chinese greet each other, they don't say, 'Hello, how are you?' but 'Have you eaten or not?' When Chinese measure population, they don't count heads, as Westerners do, but *kou,* or 'mouths.' The word for population is *ren-kou,* 'people mouths.'" Fox Butterfield, CHINA: ALIVE IN THE BITTER SEA (Bantam Books: New York, 1983), 105.

"Professor Xu / Madame Bovary / Sparrow War." I imagined Professor Xu but Chairman Mao's "Sparrow War" in 1956 was real. Scenes from that war are included in the BBC documentary *Chairman Mao: The Last Emperor*. During the Cultural Revolution "No Name Lake," *Weiming Hu* in Chinese, "was awash with lifeless, bloated bodies"— victims, directly or indirectly, of the Red Guard. See Anne F. Thurston, ENEMIES OF THE PEOPLE (133). "Language… a cracked kettle" is, of course, from Flaubert, his MADAME BOVARY.

"Sentences for Jiang Qing." 1. "China's Last Lady" has in it the much-quoted line of Jiang Qing in defense of herself at the trial of the so-called Gang of Four in 1980: viz. "I was the Chairman's dog. When he told me to bite I bit." Roxane Witke is the source of much of my information about Jiang Qing. See, for example, her book MADAME MAO: THE WHITE-BONED DEMON (Simon and Schuster: New York, 1992).

Until No Stone Is Left

"Reading Tiananmen Square." Mike O'Connor's most recent full-length collection of his own poems and translations is THE BASIN: LIFE IN A CHINESE PROVINCE (Empty Bowl: Port Townsend, 1988). COLORS OF DAYBREAK AND DUSK, a small book of his translations of Chia Tao (779–843 A.D.), was handsomely published by Tangram in 1995.

Fox Butterfield, in CHINA: ALIVE IN THE BITTER SEA, retells the story of Bai Hua's "banned-in-China film" *Bitter Love*: "Although Bai Hua was a veteran of the People's Liberation Army since the 1940s, he had been an outspoken advocate of greater freedom of expression for artists and writers. His film script told the story of a painter who returned to China after 1949, filled with patriotism and a desire to take part in the building of a new China. But during the Cultural Revolution he is harshly persecuted for his suspected foreign connections, and he finally takes refuge in a reed marsh, subsisting on raw fish. After the downfall of the radicals in 1976, he collapses in a snow-covered field and dies. His body leaves an imprint in the shape of a huge question mark. The painter makes clear his point before dying when he says, 'I love the motherland, but the motherland does not love me'" (451).

When "Small Questions" was posted, unsigned, in Tiananmen Square, it included this note from its author: "From a dialogue between a four-year-old girl and her mother." Mike O'Connor, its translator, notes: "The rainbow flower," which the mother refers to at the end of the poem, "is a flower in a child's cartoon series on Chinese television; it has magical properties and is considered highly auspicious."

Napoleon's line, "China is a sleeping giant...," has been used by practically everyone who has written about China since. Anne F. Thurston describes the events of August 18, 1966, in Tiananmen Square: the rally of "the newly formed Red Guard" and Chairman Mao's speech—"to rebel is justified"—to them (ENEMIES OF THE PEOPLE, 95–96). See Harrison Salisbury's TIANANMEN DIARY: THIRTEEN DAYS IN JUNE (Little, Brown: Boston, 1989) for both his attribution to Mao of the old Chinese saying "Don't challenge a rattlesnake..." and his reporting of the conversation he had with a Chinese student in Tiananmen Square the morning after: "one point one billion Chinese hearts are dead." Lu Xun's line—"As long as there shall be stones, the seeds of fire will not die."—gave Geremie Barmé and John Minford the title of the anthology they edited: SEEDS OF FIRE: CHINESE VOICES OF CONSCIENCE (Noonday: Boston, 1989).

It is Harrison Salisbury who says that Tiananmen Square is "the biggest public square in the world" (TIANANMEN DIARY, 12).

Thurston's comparison of Mao's Cultural Revolution to "the Nazi holocaust, the Stalinist purges, and the recent genocide in Cambodia" can be found in her ENEMY OF THE PEOPLE (xvi).

In "Mad Woman," Zhuangzi is one of the great original Daoist teachers. His dates are uncertain, but he probably lived in the fourth century B.C. His teachings are known in English as the INNER CHAPTERS.

There are many re-tellings of the Qin Shi Huang story, his burning of the books and his burying alive the intellectuals of his day, but I am referring here to Thurston's re-telling of it (21–22). The phrase "a failure of morality," having to do with the Cultural Revolution, is hers too (xix). "A rupture of conscience" belongs to Harold Laski.

Pronunciation Guide

"The pinyin system for romanizing Chinese has its origins in a system of romanization developed in Soviet east Asia in the early 1930s and employed later that decade in parts of China. With some modifications, pinyin itself was introduced by the Chinese in the 1950s. It is now the official romanization system in the People's Republic of China, has been adopted by the United Nations and other world agencies, and has become the system most commonly used in scholarship and journalism, largely supplanting the older Wade-Giles system." Jonathan D. Spence, in a note on "The Use of Pinyin," from his book THE SEARCH FOR MODERN CHINA (W.W. Norton: New York, 1990), xxv.

In Chinese *pinyin* means "spells the sounds" and, in most cases, it sounds like it looks. But there are exceptions. For example, in THE POLITICS OF MY HEART:

Consonants. *C* is pronounced *ts* (lo*ts*), as in Shen *C*ongwen. *Q* is pronounced *ch* (*ch*op), as in *Q*ufu, *Q*ing Ming, Jiang *Q*ing, *Q*in Cheng, and *Q*in Shi Huang. *X* is pronounced *sh* (*sh*are), as in *X*ue Tao, Wu Shao*x*iang, Professor *X*u, Lu *X*un, and Deng *X*iaoping. *Z* is pronounced *ds* (rea*ds*), as in Lao*z*i, *Z*aofan you li, and Zhuang*z*i. *Zh* is pronounced *j* (*j*udge), as in Shen*zh*en, *Zh*uangzi, and *Zh*ong/guo.

Vowels in pinyin mostly sound like they look too. But it is helpful to know that *e* before *n* or *ng* is pronounced *uh* (l*u*ng), as in Qin Ch*e*ng, Deng Xiaoping, Shenzh*e*n, and Shen Congw*e*n.

Spence, in his SEARCH FOR MODERN CHINA, which is the standard account of Chinese history from the late Ming dynasty (early 17th century) to and through the events in Tiananmen Square in the spring of 1989, has included: general instructions for pronouncing pinyin, a table of conversions between the Wade-Giles system and pinyin, and a glossary of Chinese names with their sounds spelled out. I recommend it, as I do Alasdair Clayre's "Note on Chinese Names and Terms" in his HEART OF THE DRAGON.

Confucius remains Confucius here, rather than becoming Kongfuzi which might make him unrecognizable in English. But the Taoist teachers Lao-tzu and Chuang-tzu in the Wade-Giles system have become the Daoist teachers Laozi and Zhuangzi in pinyin, just as the T'ang poets Tu Fu, Li Po, and Hsüeh T'ao have become the Tang poets Du Fu, Li Bai, and Xue Tao respectively. And the Song poet, essayist, and scholar Ou-yang Hsiu has become Ouyang Xiu.

from *Pleasure Boat Studio*

an essay written by Ouyang Xiu,
Song dynasty poet, essayist, and scholar,
on the twelfth day of the twelfth month
in the *renwu* year (January 25, 1043)

*I have heard of men of antiquity who fled from the world to
distant rivers and lakes and refused to their dying day to return.
They must have found some source of pleasure there. If one is
not anxious for profit, even at the risk of danger, or is not
convicted of a crime and forced to embark; rather, if one has a
favorable breeze and gentle seas and is able to rest comfortably
on a pillow and mat, sailing several hundred miles in a single
day, then is boat travel not enjoyable? Of course, I have no time
for such diversions. But since 'pleasure boat' is the designation
of boats used for such pastimes, I have now adopted it as the
name of my studio. Is there anything wrong with that?*

Translated by Ronald Egan
THE LITERARY WORKS OF OU-YANG HSIU
Cambridge University Press
New York 1984